101 Creative DATES

For Latter-day Saints

101 Creative DATES

For Latter-day Saints

Lindsey Shumway

by Lindsey Shumway

To the Fielding Children

CFI
Springville, Utah

ISBN 13: 978-1-55517-933-9
ISBN 10: 1-55517-933-9

Published by CFI, an imprint of Cedar Fort, Inc.
925 N. Main, Springville, UT, 84663
Distributed by Cedar Fort, Inc., www.cedarfort.com

LIBRARY OF CONGRESS CATALOGING-IN-PUBLICATION DATA

Shumway, Lindsey.
101 creative dates for Latter-Day Saints / by Lindsey Shumway.
p. cm.
ISBN 1-55517-933-9
1. Single people--Conduct of life. 2. Dating (Social customs)--Religious aspects--Christianity. 3. Dating (Social customs)--Religious aspects--Mormon Church. I. Title. II. Title: One hundred and one dates for Latter-Day Saints.

BV4596.S5S49 2006
241'.6765088289332--dc22

2006019043

Cover design by Nicole Williams
Cover design © 2006 by Lyle Mortimer
Printed in the United States of America

10 9 8 7 6 5 4 3 2 1

Printed on acid-free paper

Dedication

To my husband, Adam, who used to call me his eternal companion candidate. I'm so glad I got the job!

Acknowledgments

My good parents, Stan and Cathy Jex, made sure I didn't go on any dates until I was sixteen. Their insistence inspired me to make sure that my dates were not wasted once I was finally allowed to go. I had three dates on my sixteenth birthday, and it just got better from there. I appreciate my parents' love, support, and counsel throughout my dating years. My siblings, Christopher, Benjamin, Jeremiah, and Jennifer, have always been supportive. I will forever appreciate their examples, honesty, and love.

My best friend growing up, who became my confidant when we were ten years old, made all the double dates possible. Becca Loughran Cartier is one of the most creative people I know. She was, and is, the kind of best friend every girl should have—fun, energetic, outgoing, and positive. Many of the dates in this book are derived from our conversations during silly sleepovers and weekend shopping trips to thrift stores.

No creative date is possible without a fabulous guy who is willing to play along. I would like to recognize a few who were particularly exceptional for the part they played in helping me enjoy each and every date I ever went on. A special thanks to Jeff Walls, Doug Merrill, David Arp, Ryan Bean, Jonathan Filmore, and Aidan Kennedy; your wives are lucky gals. To Ralph, thanks for teaching me everything you know about pickup lines and for letting me use them on you occasionally.

The talented staff at Cedar Fort deserve a medal for all the patience, effort, diligent work, and tireless support that they give to every one of their authors, including me.

Table of Contents

How to Use This Book

THIS BOOK IS SIMPLE to use. These creative dates are categorized by theme and are easy to skim through. Flip around until you find something that looks interesting and then start planning.

Date descriptions provide helpful guides for "creative elements" you can choose from to create the perfect theme date. "Movie Lovers" gives you great suggestions for movies that will fit each date's theme. "Overachievers" will love the suggestions added to each date that explain what you can do to go above and beyond to really impress your date. You'll also find periodic "Warnings!" that will give you helpful suggestions for making the date work out well. All of the 101 creative dates can be ramped up or tapered down to fit into any budget.

Need a date that meets specific requirements? Check out the easy-to-use icons on each date, showing you which dates are Good for First Dates, Great in Any Weather, and Good for a Group.

GOOD FOR FIRST DATES

GREAT IN ANY WEATHER

GOOD FOR A GROUP

Last, for a simple alphabetical list of all the Creative Dates, see the index. You can also refer to the appendix for a talk by Elder Dallin H. Oaks to understand why dating is so important in preparing for your future.

Chapter 1:

Creative Dating 101

Why Date Creatively?

DO YOU EVER HAVE a free Friday night when you and all your friends meet at someone's house and inevitably ask the question, "So what do you want to do tonight?" The answer rarely changes. "I don't know, what do you want to do?" Most people don't have spontaneously fabulous answers to that question, and that's why I wrote this book. Whether you're sixteen or forty-six, creative dating will help you turn those available hours into your favorite adventures. Instead of just hanging out this weekend, why not make a memory that you'll rave about for the rest of your life? Below are the reasons that you—and everyone else—should take the TIME to date creatively:

T. Thrilling change of pace!
I. Inexpensive!
M. Memorable!
E. Experience each other!

Thrilling change of pace. Aren't you getting tired of hanging out or simply doing the same old dinner and a movie routine? Participating in a creative date will spark the energy within you. It's time to turn up the notch on your weekend and try something new.

Inexpensive. Enjoyable dating doesn't require a filet mignon and the opera every weekend. You can have flair and cultural inspiration with just ten dollars and a few simple ideas from this book. Your date is going to appreciate all the time and thought you put into planning the date, not the hundreds of dollars you spend trying to impress.

Memorable. Making memories is important. What happens if your date is lackluster? You might not get a second date, or your spouse may decide to play X-box with friends next weekend. Give your date a night to remember.

Experience each other. Get to know your date; ask your date to take a chance and try something silly or ridiculous. Learn how your date reacts in unusual situations. Find out if this is a person you'd be willing to spend another four to six hours with. Show your date who you really are and how creative you can be.

The Three P's of Dating

IN ELDER DALLIN H. OAKS'S MAY 2005 CES fireside, he mentioned the three p's of dating. In order for an activity to be a date, it must include all three p's: planned ahead, paid for, and paired off.

Planned Ahead. Planning your dates ahead of time is an excellent idea for many reasons. 1. It allows you to resolve any up-front concerns that your date may have. 2. It gives you an opportunity to make a good impression by showing your date that you have been looking forward to your time together. 3. It eliminates any awkward moments of not knowing what to do. 4. It allows you to feel comfortable and prepared for what the date will bring.

Paid For. It is a widely accepted fact that men pay for dates. This is a good practice. Men need to develop a habit of taking care of and providing for the women in their life. For men, making necessary arrangements for money before a date and reassuring your date that you have it covered is a great practice; it lets everyone know where the responsibilities lie from the beginning.

Paired Off. Pairing off is not as scary as it seems. Just because you have a specific date doesn't mean you are exclusive; rather, it means you have each other's exclusive attention for one evening. There are many advantages to dating this way. For example, it allows you to experience your date on a level that allows you to get past their exterior. Also, you will have a dedicated partner in all activities, and it ultimately leads to deeper bonds and deeper trust.

Keep the three p's in mind when planning your dates, and your dating experiences will be satisfying and enjoyable.

General Creative Dating Suggestions

EACH CHAPTER IN THIS book is designed to give you specific ideas you can use to have creative dating experiences; however, it is impossible to write every dating idea in one book. When you get to the point that you feel like trying out your own ideas, here are some basic guidelines:

- Buy, make, or eat food.
- Visit a place of interest.
- Learn something new.

- Give a gift to each other or someone else.
- Use a theme and theme-based invitations.
- Involve a parent or relative.
- Watch a theme-related movie.
- Play or watch a game or sport.
- Plan a surprise.
- Involve costumes or special dressing instructions.
- Give service.
- Participate in or watch a performing art.
- Make a tangible item together.
- Take pictures to create lasting memories.
- Learn about each other as much as possible.
- Try some pickup lines.

Pickup Lines

I HAVE A PASSION for cheesy pickup lines. I've used hundreds myself; some worked, some didn't. I believe the only value a pickup line has is to get the person you use it on to crack up laughing or to give you a chance. Pickup lines should never be used to manipulate others.

When my husband and I were getting to know each other, he used a pickup line on me that won me over because it was complimentary, of course, but also because it was creative. I was preparing to leave for my senior prom. Adam was an acquaintance at the time. He took one look at me and said, "Lindsey, do you have your cell phone?" I gave him a quizzical look and said, "Why would I need a cell phone at senior prom?" He kept a completely straight face as he said, "Well, Lindsey, you look so good that when your date sees you, he's going to pass out, and someone's going to have to call 911." He's had my attention ever since.

Unfortunately, most people don't have quite the talent for off-the-cuff pickup lines that my husband has. Here are a few that you might find fun and useful:

- Can I borrow a quarter? [Why?] I want to call my mom and tell her that I found the girl of my dreams.
- What does it feel like to be the most beautiful girl in the room?
- There must be something wrong with my eyes because I can't take them off you.

- Hi, I'm Mr. Right. Someone said you were looking for me.
- Do you believe in love at first sight, or should I walk by again?
- Aside from being hot, what other talents do you have?
- Are you accepting applications for your fan club?
- Are you as beautiful on the inside as you are on the outside?
- Are you going to kiss me, or do I have to lie to my diary?
- Aren't we supposed to get together later tonight for a candlelight dinner?
- Are your legs tired? They've been running through my mind all day!
- You're so sweet that you're going to put Hershey's out of business.
- Can I get a picture of you? I need to show Santa what I want for Christmas.
- Would you do me a favor and tell your boyfriend that he's a lucky guy.
- Did you have Campbell's soup today? Because you are lookin' mmm . . . mmm . . . good.
- Do you eat a lot of Lucky Charms? You look magically delicious.
- Do you mind if I stare at you up close instead of from across the room?
- Excuse me, I may be lost. Could you give me directions to wherever you're going?
- Do beautiful eyes run in your family?
- Wait! Don't walk into that building! The sprinklers might go off!
- Don't you know me from somewhere?
- Good evening, may a thorn sit down among the roses?
- Have you always been this cute, or did you have to work on it?
- Hey, kitten, how about spending some of your nine lives on me?
- Don't I know you? Oh yeah, you're the girl (or guy) with the gorgeous smile.

- Hi, I need your help. My mom says that if I don't get a date by tomorrow she's going to put me up for adoption!
- Hi, my name's Right . . . Mr. Right.
- How's your fever? [What fever?] Oh, you just look super hot to me!
- I believe it was Socrates who said, "Know thyself." Well, I already know myself; how about I get to know you?
- I can read palms. [Write your phone number on the person's hand.] It says you're going to call me later!
- I didn't know angels could fly so low!
- I didn't know that Miss America lived here!
- I envy your lipstick.
- I hear you have a good dentist. Mind if I check out his work?
- Is your name Gillette? You're the best a man can get.
- It must be dark outside—all the sunshine is right in this room!
- It's my birthday! How about a birthday kiss? [Is it really your birthday?] No, but why don't you give me a birthday kiss anyway?
- Let's make like a fabric softener and snuggle.
- Life without you would be like a broken pencil—pointless.
- Well, here I am. What were your other two wishes?
- What's your first name? Hmm, that sounds good with my last name.
- When God made you he was showing off.
- You're so sweet that I'm getting a toothache just looking at you.
- You might be asked to leave soon. [Why?] You're making all the other ladies look bad.
- You look beautiful today—just like every other day.
- You see my friend over there? [Friend waves.] He wants to know if you think I'm cute.
- You're so hot you'd make the devil sweat.

Creative Invitations

- Buy a small puzzle. Put it together and write your request on the back. Then take it apart and put it back in the box. Leave it on your prospective date's doorstep with a note to call you when it's put together.
- Buy a balloon bouquet and put a few words of your invitation on small pieces of paper inside each balloon. Write, "Pop Me," on each one. The last part should say something like, "I'd feel lighter than air if you said yes."
- Buy a bouquet of Tootsie Pop suckers and attach a note that invites your date out by saying, "You'd be a Sucker to say no! Call me!"
- With the help of Mom or a roommate, get permission to enter your date's room and dump a bag of Hershey kisses on the bedroom floor with a note that says, "I Kiss the ground you walk on" and invites them out.
- Take your date a bag of Swedish fish and attach a note that says, "Of all the fish in sea, you're the one for me!" (You might even try using a live fish also.)
- Bake your date a cake, frost your invitation on top, and leave the cake on the doorstep.
- Take a box of Lucky Charms to your date with a note attached that says, "I would be so Lucky to have you as my date" and explains the details.
- Cut up circles of different colors and sizes. Tape them all over your date's room, house, or car. Then, on a sign or a big circle, write, "I hate to put you on the spot, but will go out on a date with me?" You could do the same thing with hearts and write, "I'd have a heart attack if you'd go out with me."
- Attach a laminated picture of yourself to a string. Then take a big pot and fill it with water. Put the picture in the middle of the water (use the string to keep it in place), and freeze it. When it's frozen solid, take it out of the pot and put it on your date's

doorstep or somewhere that your date will see it before it melts. Attach a note or sign that says, "To break the ice, I thought it would be nice if you would go out with me."

- Buy a hefty stack of paper plates. Write one word on each plate, asking your date out. After writing your invitation, cover the plate stack with chocolate frosting to make it look like a real cake. Deliver it to your date and have someone standing nearby with a camera!
- Create a scavenger hunt. Make up your own clues that lead your date on a funny journey searching for you. Be ready with a dozen roses to ask out your date when you're found.
- Decorate your date's locker or car with a huge poster asking for a date.
- String toilet paper outside your date's door, criss-crossing it in front of the entrance. Write your message on the paper for your date to see upon leaving in the morning.
- Make a fake label for a two-liter bottle of soda. Write a message that says, "I'd be soda-lighted if you'd go out with me." Then give the bottle to your date.
- Hire one of your younger siblings to show up at your date's doorstep and sing, "You are so beautiful to me," *Little Rascals* style. Have your sibling pass your date a note that says, "Will you go out with [your name]? Check yes or no."

Icebreakers and Get-to-Know-You Games

WHEN YOU GET a group of people together, even if it's only four, sometimes you need to break the ice. You want to encourage people to let their guard down a little and feel more comfortable. Here are some terrific icebreakers and games that are fun to use to get a date started right.

GROUP JUGGLING

Use balls, beanbags, scarves, or anything you can find. As you juggle together, you'll learn the names of those you're throwing things to.

MAD GAB

This is a game that has funky phrases jumbled together. The group's goal is to figure out the popular phrase that is jumbled up. This game promotes laughter and hilarious confusion.

THE STORY OF MY NAME

Take turns telling how you came to have your particular name. Were you named after an ancestor? A famous person?

TABOO

This is a game in which you giving your partner verbal clues so that he can guess the word you're describing. The catch is you can't use a few "taboo" words. This game teaches you to speak up and think quickly!

TWO TRUTHS AND ONE LIE

Every person gets a piece of paper and, without showing anyone, writes down three things about himself—two of them true and one false. The object is to fool everyone into thinking the lies are the truth and the truths are the lie. You'll learn a lot about each other—things you wouldn't find out any other way.

LOADED QUESTIONS

This is a nationally produced game that reveals people's true feelings about tough subjects. It's a blast with strangers.

BLINDFOLDED NIGHTTIME OBSTACLE COURSE

Wait until it's dark, set up an obstacle course, and lead your date through it with a blindfold on. This builds trust and allows you to feel comfortable being closer to each other.

THE NAME POEM

All players write their name in a vertical line on a piece of paper. Take a few minutes and write words that describe you next to each letter of your name. For a fun and challenging spin on this game, after you write your name down trade papers with your date so that your date is describing you! Share what you write.

PANTOMIME

Create a list of things you'd like to know about each other, such as your job, favorite food, college major, and so on. Have each person in the group pantomime these items while everyone else guesses.

THE M&M GAME

Get a big bag of M&M's and a cheap bowl from a local thrift store. Divide the M&M's evenly among everyone who is playing and place the bowl in the middle of the players. Go around the circle and have everyone tell one thing they've done in their life. For each thing you say, add one M&M to the bowl. If anyone else has done the same thing, they get to add an M&M to the bowl. The goal is to get all your M&M's in the bowl first; whoever runs out of candy first gets the bowl full of candy.

Dates Under Ten Dollars

MEMORABLE DATES DON'T have to cost a fortune. Use some of these handy ideas the next time you are a little low on funds.

1. Go for a bike ride.
2. Swing at the park.
3. Race toy trains.
4. Go rollerblading.
5. Go on a scavenger hunt.
6. Make kites and fly them.
7. Visit a fish hatchery.
8. Throw your date a surprise party during the date.
9. Throw Frisbees.
10. Wash each other's car.
11. Pull homemade taffy.
12. Take kids to the park.
13. Attend a free concert or exhibit.
14. Set up a candlelight dinner in your backyard.
15. Go fishing.

16. Go to general conference.
17. Make mud pies and have a fight.
18. Play croquet.
19. Make a home movie.
20. Make thank-you cards for your date's parents.
21. Build a giant sundae on top of a cookie sheet.
22. Create snow sculptures.
23. Take a dog for a walk.
24. Plant or weed a garden.
25. Do a paint-by-numbers or color a fuzzy poster.
26. Take a portable TV and VCR or DVD player onto your roof and watch movies at night.
27. Make a fort out of blankets and pillows, and look through yearbooks with flashlights.
28. Play hide-and-seek in the mall.
29. Catch frogs and race them.
30. Collect bugs and grasshoppers (this is especially fun with children).
31. Go to a library and read together.
32. Go for a walk on a cold night and make hot cocoa.
33. Play games at an arcade.
34. Star gaze at a planetarium.
35. See an IMAX movie matinee.
36. Share a funnel cake at a local fair or festival.
37. Have a picnic at a park.
38. Float down a river on inner tubes.
39. Go to a café that features live music.
40. Have a water fight with Super Soakers or water balloons.
41. Take a walk on the beach.
42. Take a ride on a bicycle built for two.
43. Go to a dog show.
44. Make and eat ice cream sundaes.
45. Go to a book reading or lecture.
46. Play an old board game.
47. Build a sand castle.
48. Cook a Dutch oven dessert
49. Cheer on a mutual friend who is competing in an event.
50. Check out classic LDS DVDs from the Church library.

Chapter 2:

Artistic Dates

date one

The Painting Date

The Idea

TO EXPERIMENT WITH a pallet full of painting options.

Creative Elements

HAVE THE GUYS paint the girls' toenails. Try finger painting or painting with your toes. Get a watercolor set and try to paint the same item. Paint one of the walls in your room a unique color. Take a painting class together at a local do-it-yourself hardware store; free classes are offered all the time. Do paint by the numbers. Find a ceramics store and paint your mothers a present.

Movie Lovers

WATCH *What Dreams May Come*

Overachievers

GO TO AN art exhibit or gallery. Buy a canvas and create a masterpiece together.

date two

The Shakespearean Date

The Idea

ADD A LITTLE drama to your life.

Creative Elements

READ SOME OF Shakespeare's sonnets to each other and then go to a local production of a Shakespearean play. Dress up in Old English attire and have a sword fight. Put on a miniplay for your friends or family members. Find a local theater that is holding auditions and try out for a part together.

Movie Lovers

WATCH A modern movie that uses Shakespeare's work as a theme, such as *10 Things I Hate about You, A Midsummer Night's Dream, Romeo and Juliet, Hamlet,* and *Much Ado about Nothing.*

Overachievers

GO TO THE nearest big city and see a major production of a Shakespearean work. Buy your date a copy of your favorite play by Shakespeare as a memento of the evening.

date three

The Redecorating Date

The Idea

GET TO KNOW your date better while playing around in your date's personal space.

Creative Elements

WATCH A HOME-DECORATING show or read a magazine to get ideas for your project. Find inexpensive ways to change the feel of the room, such as a new rug, throw pillows, and organizational items that will help eliminate clutter. Clean off every flat surface. Wash the windows. Find a new scent for the room that works for your date (like vanilla or melon), use air fresheners, carpet fresheners, or potpourri and candles to create just the right feel. Change the lighting by uncovering windows, adding mirrors, cleaning old fixtures, or adding a new lamp.

Overachievers

TO MAKE THE date unforgettable, buy a coordinating picture frame for a photo of the two of you.

Warning! After a few hours of this, most guys will need a reward for all their hard work; be creative and reward them creatively.

date four

The Sculpture Date

The Idea

MOLD AND SHAPE your evening while you explore sculpting.

Creative Elements

BUY MOLDING CLAY and create funny works of art. Read or look through a book on how to sculpt or one about a famous sculptor. Visit a museum and check out other people's creations; feel them with your hands, if it is permitted, while imagining what it would be like to have shaped the piece yourself. Play the game *Cranium;* one of the sections in the game includes creating sculptures. Take a pottery class or mold something using a potter's wheel.

Movie Lovers

WATCH *Ghost.*

Overachievers

AFTER CREATING YOUR piece of art, take it to a furnace, have it fired, and give it to your date as a gift.

date five

The Music Appreciation Date

The Idea

GET TO KNOW your date's musical likes and dislikes and try out some new tunes.

Creative Elements

BRING YOUR FAVORITE CDs, and tell your date to do the same. Listen to them throughout the evening. Burn a sound track for your date, including some songs from your CDs and some from your date's. This can be done with MP3 players as well. Go to a concert or recital; a child's performance can be fun. If either of you play an instrument, give your date a miniconcert. Go to a music store and try out musical instruments, and listen to demos of CDs you would normally overlook.

Movie Lovers

WATCH *Sound of Music, Phantom of the Opera,* or *Grease.*

Overachievers

TAKE A CLASS together and learn to play an instrument, like the guitar or piano. Go to a restaurant that has musicians playing while you dine.

date six

The Antiquities Date

The Idea

DISCOVER *NEW* THINGS about your date while you are learning about things that are *old*.

Creative Elements

GO TO AN ancient history museum, and explore the fossils. Make your own fossils by stamping things into plaster or cement. Visit an antiques store, and see who can find the coolest item for under ten dollars. Visit a local historical site that has petroglyphs or other interesting Native American art. Learn how to antique a piece of furniture.

LEARN ABOUT ANCIENT Egypt. Write messages with symbols, and put together a treasure hunt with clues.

Movie Lovers

WATCH *Jurassic Park, National Treasure, The Mummy,* or *The Mummy Returns.*

Overachievers

ANTIQUE A PIECE of furniture.

date seven

The Crafty Date

The Idea

CRAFT YOUR DATE'S positive opinion of you!

Creative Elements

MAKE A SCRAPBOOK page about your date. Tie a quilt for charity. Make a silk or fresh flower arrangement, and give it to your date to take home. Teach your date how to sew something useful, like a pillowcase. Whittle a walking stick, and then use it to go for a hike. Try tying different useful knots. Stencil a design on an otherwise generic object. Make boondoggle key chains. Make a model. Paint a figurine. Do a Shrinky Dink.

Overachievers

ASK A STAINED glass artist to show you how to make a stained glass window, or learn how to blow glass.

Warning! Try to throw in at least one feminine craft and one masculine craft. Make sure everyone tries something new.

date eight

The Writing Date

The Idea

WIN YOUR DATE over with words.

Creative Elements

BRAINSTORM A COOL story together and draw stick illustrations for it. Write poems about each other. Check out a calligraphy book from the library and mimic the styles shown. Create an alphabet book together and give it a creative theme, like the sporting alphabet, the Mormon alphabet, or even the sci-fi alphabet. Play *Scrabble* or *Boggle*. Do crossword puzzles together. Create a jigsaw puzzle about yourselves—one person gets the across questions, the other gets the down questions. Write a name poem about yourself or your date, and share them when you're done. Take a paragraph from a work of Shakespeare, and translate it into modern English or slang.

Movie Lovers

WATCH *Finding Forrester*.

Overachievers

BEFORE THE DATE, write a poem about your date or about the two of you together. Have it framed and give it to your date as a gift. Write a children's book together and submit it to a publisher.

date nine

The Opera Date

The Idea

DISCOVER WHAT IT feels like to sing at the top of your lungs.

Creative Elements

LISTEN TO AN opera CD. (I love the Opera Babes.) Learn about some of the opera greats: Verdi, Puccini, Mozart, and others. Attend an opera at a college or university. Sing along at the top of your lungs with the radio in your car.

Movie Lovers

WATCH ANY OPERA on DVD.

Overachievers

GO TO AN opera, but research the story line beforehand so you and your date can follow along more easily. Dress up!

Warning! Don't surprise your date with this idea; some people hate opera.

date ten

The Museum Date

The Idea

DISCOVER THE TRUE meaning of fine art.

Creative Elements

VISIT A LOCAL museum. Slowly explore every exhibit, pointing out anything interesting you notice. Be quiet. Take a sketch pad and try to draw a sculpture you see. Dine in the museum café. Research online the art you saw at the museum. Discover the story behind the art.

Movie Lovers

WATCH *The Mummy* or *The Mummy Returns.*

Overachievers

GET TICKETS TO a special exhibit or museum event.

date eleven

The Carpentry Date

The Idea

TO BUILD THE date on a solid foundation.

Creative Elements

PLAY WITH BUILDING blocks together. Build an elaborate system of dominoes. Find a book at the local library that has a project that looks like fun, and make it together. Gather together hammers, wood, nails, screws, and any other tools you may need to create any project you choose. You could construct a shadow box or simple bookshelves.

Movie Lovers

WATCH *The Money Pit* or *Mr. Blandings Builds His Dreamhouse.*

Overachievers

MAKE A DOLLHOUSE and donate it to a children's hospital or homeless shelter.

Warning! Don't overdo it with the power tools; we don't want this to turn into the Hospital Date!

date twelve

The Recycled Art Date

The Idea

SEE WHAT THE two of you can make out of nothing.

Creative Elements

PIECE TOGETHER A mosaic out of broken tiles. Use recyclable items to create something decorative. Collect useless rubbish from around your house, and see who can come up with the most fabulous plan for what it could be turned into. Then make the dream a reality.

Movie Lovers

WATCH *Robots.*

Overachievers

TRY TO CREATE something with moving parts.

date thirteen

The Make Your Own Movie Date

4+

The Idea

WRITE, DIRECT, AND star in your own movie.

Creative Elements

WRITE A SCRIPT together, pick out costumes, and then use a camcorder to film your scenes. You can film part of your movie with your camera phone for a lasting keepsake. Add a sound track to your movie. Invite friends and family over to watch your minimasterpiece.

Movie Lovers

WATCH *King Kong* to get inspiration.

Overachievers

MAKE THIS AN ongoing date over the course of a few weeks. Use your computer to edit and clean up the production.

Chapter 3:

Competitive Dates

date fourteen

The Golf Date

4+

The Idea

TO DISCOVER IF your caddie is a real candidate.

Creative Elements

WEAR POLO SHIRTS and visors. Play a round of miniature golf. Have a picnic near a putting green. (Watch out for errant shots, however.) Hit a bucket of balls at the driving range. Teach your date how to golf. Go just outside the golf course and look for lost balls. Try a virtual golf simulator at a sporting goods store. Play *Tiger Woods PGA Tour 2006* on PS2 or XBOX. Play Frisbee golf.

Movie Lovers

WATCH *The Greatest Game Ever Played* or *The Legend of Bagger Vance.*

Overachievers

HAVE A MEAL at the country club. Play a round of eighteen holes, playing best-ball so everyone has a good time.

Warning! A golf course can be a pretty serious place; you can have fun, but remember to be courteous to other golfers who are trying to concentrate.

The Bowling Date

4+

The Idea

LET THE GOOD times roll as you bowl.

Creative Elements

GET TEN TWO-LITER bottles of soda and set them up like bowling pins on a flat surface. Use a watermelon for the bowling ball, and see how many pins you can knock over in ten frames. Eventually the melon will bust open, and that's when you use the ball and the pins to have a sticky, messy food fight. Go to a bowling alley and try whacky variations of bowling, like eyes closed with bumpers, granny style only, boys against girls, or couple versus couple. Go to late-night disco bowling. Get a kit and try lawn bowling. Watch a bowling tournament on TV.

Overachievers

JOIN A BOWLING league together. Ask a league bowler to give you pointers.

Warning! If you decide to do watermelon bowling, make sure everyone brings a change of clothes. Having access to a couple of nearby showers is a great idea as well.

date sixteen

The Water Date

4+

The Idea

CHILL OUT TOGETHER on a hot day.

Creative Elements

GO TO A lake or pool and have underwater Olympics. See who can hold their breath the longest, who can swim the farthest under water, who can dive to the bottom to grab an item, and who can do the best handstand. Afterward, play Twister. Get water guns and water grenades and have a water battle. This is the most fun when it's a surprise attack! Set up a net and play water balloon volleyball using beach towels.

Movie Lovers

WATCH *Water World* or *Blue Crush.*

Overachievers

INCORPORATE ALL THE same Creative Elements at a water park.

Warning! Not everyone feels comfortable in front of others in a swimming suit, so make sure everyone is okay before you spend a lot of time planning.

date seventeen

The "Who's the Man?" Date

4+

The Idea

PIT ALL THE male daters against each other in an alpha male competition.

Creative Elements

PUT TOGETHER A list of tasks that all the boys will have to complete. Girls get clipboards and are the judges. Whoever wins gets a gift certificate to some place that all guys love. Some ideas for activities to include are:

Who can scarf down five hamburgers the fastest? Who can chop a piece of wood the fastest? Go to a local elementary school and set up an obstacle course using the kiddy toys; see who can get through the fastest. See who can fold a pair of pants the best. See who can solve a math problem the fastest. Give them a tough word to spell and see who can get it right. There a hundreds of ideas you could use for this. Be creative!

Overachievers

ADD WHO CAN give the best five-second kiss?

Warning! Make sure that each girl is always cheering for her man, whether or not he is the winner.

date eighteen

The Bigger and Better Date

4+

The Idea

ONE-UPPING YOUR FRIENDS can be fun.

Creative Elements

EACH COUPLE GETS a penny. You split up and take the penny door to door, asking for something bigger and better. You keep going from house to house until you feel like you have something great. (Make sure the people giving you things know they will not be getting their items back.) Set a time limit; usually thirty minutes is sufficient. When you all get back, compare who has the biggest and best item.

Warning! Be prepared for some homeowners who are not interested in playing along.

date nineteen

The Fun and Games Date

The Idea

GET TO KNOW your date's inner child.

Creative Elements

BUILD SOMETHING TOGETHER out of Legos, play with Barbies and GI Joes, put a puzzle together, play any kiddy games, like Hi-Ho Cheerio! or Chutes and Ladders. Play on a backyard swing set, watch cartoons, or play dress-up. Turn everything into a competition, just like children do, by seeing who can finish first or who can build the best Lego airplane or who can swing the highest.

Movie Lovers

WATCH *Toy Story* or *Toy Story 2.*

Overachievers

BEFORE THE DATE, ask your date's parents what your date's favorite toy was as a child. Buy one and surprise your date with it.

Chapter 4:

Foreign Dates

date twenty

The Polynesian Date

The Idea

PLAY POLYNESIAN STYLE.

Creative Elements

GET A GOOD island CD to set the right tone. Wear grass skirts, and teach each other to hula. Eat tropical fruit, like mangoes, papayas, kiwi fruit, bananas, and pineapples. Share a Hawaiian pizza. Use made-up airline tickets as invitations, including things like arrival and departure times, seat numbers or directions "next to me" and meals to be served. Have a hula hoop contest.

Movie Lovers

WATCH A MOVIE about the islands of the Pacific, like *The Other Side of Heaven, 50 First Dates, Blue Crush, South Pacific,* or the classic *Johnny Lingo.*

Overachievers

HAVE A ROASTED pig for dinner. Take your date surfing. Throw a luau.

date twenty-one

The French Date

The Idea

ENJOY AN EXPERIENCE culturale!

Creative Elements

MAKE YOUR DATE crepes for breakfast. Take a virtual tour of the Louvre. Go to a sidewalk café and write in your journals. Learn how to make a gourmet French pastry together, make them, and serve them to your families. Eat imported cheese and crackers with sparkling juice. Check out a CD from the library that teaches French, and learn some phrases you can say to each other.

Movie Lovers

WATCH *French Kiss, An American in Paris, Les Miserables,* or *The Scarlet Pimpernel.*

Overachievers

SEE A PRODUCTION of *Les Miserables.* Take your date to an authentic French restaurant.

date twenty-two

The Japanese Date

The Idea

EXPERIENCE JAPAN, RIGHT here in the USA.

Creative Elements

VISIT A BUDDHIST temple. Make each other stir-fry for dinner—half of the fun is all the chopping. Take a karate class. Go to a Japanese garden and walk around. Dress in a kimono, and serve your date tea. Respectfully discuss your ancestors. Eat with chopsticks. Try a Japanese steak house where the chefs do the cooking in front of you.

Movie Lovers

WATCH A JAPANESE anime movie. Watch *Shogun, The Karate Kid.*

Overachievers

GO TO A sushi bar for dinner. Try something crazy; you just might like it.

date twenty-three

The English Date

The Idea

TO HAVE A jolly good time together.

Creative Elements

EAT TEA AND crumpets. Listen to a CD by the Beatles, Spice Girls, or Alex Boye. Read passages from classic works by Shakespeare, C. S. Lewis, or Charles Dickens. Dress up in medieval costumes and have a sword fight. Google the "Crown Jewels" and learn about the monarchy. Eat bangers and mash or fish and chips. Play rugby or go to a rugby game.

Movie Lovers

WATCH *A Knight's Tale, Robin Hood, Prince of Thieves, Notting Hill,* or *Monte Python and the Holy Grail.*

Overachievers

GO TO A discotheque.

date twenty-four

The Canadian Date

The Idea

TO GIVE YOUR date a great time, eh?

Creative Elements

PLAY ROLLER HOCKEY or go to a professional hockey game between a U.S. team and a Canadian team. Learn to say, "Hello, my name is ________ " in French. Make sure you say "eh?" after everything. Go curling.

Movie Lovers

WATCH *Anne of Green Gables* or *Canadian Bacon*.

Overachievers

IF YOU LIVE close enough to the border, take a road trip to Canada. If you have an ice rink nearby, play ice hockey.

date twenty-five

The Chinese Date

The Idea

TO CREATE POSITIVE chi between you and your date.

Creative Elements

READ THE CHILDREN'S book *Rikki Tikki Tembo,* and talk about the lessons you learn from it. Go to the zoo and check out the panda bears. Make a centerpiece with bamboo in it. Learn how to spell your names in Chinese characters. Find out which animal you are on the Chinese lunar calendar; discover what this means about you. Study a book about feng shui.

Movie Lovers

WATCH *Rush Hour, Mulan,* or *Crouching Tiger, Hidden Dragon.*

Overachievers

GIVE YOUR DATE a jade piece of jewelry and explain all the symbolism behind jade. Go to a nice Chinese restaurant, and make sure to share your fortune cookies with each other at the end.

date twenty-six

The Mexican Date

The Idea

TO HAVE AN unforgettable fiesta together.

Creative Elements

MAKE HOMEMADE GUACAMOLE and pico de gallo with corn chips. Play soccer. Learn about the conquistadores who settled Mexico. Learn why Mexico celebrates Cinco de Mayo. Wear sombreros and bright colors. Listen to a CD by a Mexican artist.

Movie Lovers

WATCH *The Mask of Zorro, The Alamo,* or *The Three Amigos.*

Overachievers

TAKE YOUR DATE out to a nice Mexican restaurant. If you are close enough to the border, go for a road trip to Mexico.

The Irish Date

The Idea

MAKE A GREAT impression on your favorite lad or lass.

Creative Elements

MAKE DINNER USING lots of potatoes. Hunt for four-leaf clovers. Set up a scavenger hunt to find the pot of gold at the end of the rainbow. Wear green, orange, and white clothing. Visit a cathedral. Try your arms at hurling.

Movie Lovers

WATCH *Far and Away* or *Circle of Friends*.

Overachievers

A FEW DAYS later have your clover laminated or framed, and give it to your date. Take your date to *Riverdance*.

The Russian Date

The Idea

GET YOUR DATE to warm up to you.

Creative Elements

MAKE BORSCH OR cold cabbage soup. Go to a park and play chess like Russian masters. Take Russian pastries to your babushka. Learn how to say a funny Russian phrase like, "Your mother wears combats boots." Read *Anna Karenina* and talk about it during your date.

Movie Lovers

WATCH *Fiddler on the Roof, Anastasia, Rocky 4,* or *The Hunt for Red October.*

Overachievers

GO TO A production of *The Fiddler on the Roof.*

The World Traveler Date

The Idea

ENJOY GLOBE-TROTTING RIGHT from your own PC.

Creative Elements

TAKE A PICTURE with your date as if you were posing in front of a famous location. Once you have a great photo, find pictures from around the world that you can insert your image onto. Some places you could consider are:

The Eiffel Tower in Paris, Big Ben in London, Red Square in Russia, a tropical beach in Hawaii, or anywhere else you'd like to go. As you do this you can share with your date all the places you'd like to travel to in the future or all the places you have already visited. Research the next trip you want to take. Figure out prices, main attractions, and the best places to eat.

Movie Lovers

WATCH *An American in Paris,* any of the episodes of *Alias,* or *Around the World in 80 Days.*

Overachievers

MAKE A PHOTO album with the pictures you create.

Chapter 5:

Girly Dates

date thirty

The Day Spa Date

4+

The Idea

PAMPER YOURSELF AND your date.

Creative Elements

GIVE EACH OTHER a manicure or pedicure, with or without polish. Use hot wax to shape each other's eyebrows. Dye each other's hair or give each other scalp massages. Use mud masks. Moisturize. Play a relaxing CD of natural sounds in the background. Set up a rock fountain.

Movie Lovers

WATCH *Beauty Shop* or *Clueless.*

Overachievers

BUY A PARAFFIN waxing warmer; use it to make your hands silky.

date thirty-one

The Cookie Date

The Idea

USE SUGAR AND flour to get more out of each hour.

Creative Elements

PICK YOUR TWO favorite cookie recipes. Write down a list of ingredients and split up into two teams. See which team can scavenge the necessary items for the recipe first. Bring everything home and bake the cookies together. Leave cookies on the door of the neighbors who gave you ingredients.

Overachievers

THE NEXT DAY, go to the mall and buy a big cookie from Mrs. Fields. Have a message written on the cookie for your date, saying what a good time you had or thanking your date for coming. Leave it on your date's doorstep. Send your date a cookie bouquet, available from specialty bakeries.

date thirty-two

The Babysitting Date

The Idea

DISCOVER HOW YOUR date feels about kids.

Creative Elements

ASK A COUPLE WHO has kids if you can watch their children with a date while they go out on a date. After you get permission, bring your date along babysitting. Play with the kids, read them books, watch silly kid movies, cook them a meal, help them clean up their rooms, and make sure they say their prayers with you before they go to bed.

Movie Lovers

WATCH *Adventures in Babysitting.*

Overachievers

BRING A REGULAR movie along and perhaps some goodies. After the kids are in bed, surprise your date with your treats and movie.

Warning! Since you will probably be alone for a while on this date, make sure you are eighteen before you set up something like this.

date thirty-three

The Makeover Date

The Idea

GIVE YOUR DATE an extreme makeover.

Creative Elements

GO TO A department or thrift store and try on different outfits until you each find one that the other thinks looks great. The objective should be for each of you to end the date with at least one new outfit. Do the same with perfume and cologne. Get a haircut together; pick out the style and color together. For the girl, go to the makeup counter and get some ideas for new colors being used this season.

Movie Lovers

WATCH *My Big Fat Greek Wedding, She's All That, Princess Diaries,* or *Shallow Hal.*

Overachievers

SAME IDEA, JUST wear dressy clothes instead of everyday clothes. Try on gowns and suits.

Warning! Make sure your date knows that you care about more than just what a person looks like on the outside.

date thirty-four

The Dancing Date

4+

The Idea

DANCE THE NIGHT away, like Cinderella and Prince Charming.

Creative Elements

TAKE A DANCE class together, or put on your favorite kind of music—jazz, hip-hop, ballroom, swing, whatever—and create your own dance. Show off your moves at the next church dance. Go to a dance performance or recital. Participate in a festival with folk dancing. Go to a luau and see Polynesian dancing. Participate in your local LDS dance festival.

Movie Lovers

WATCH *Strictly Ballroom, Swing Kids,* or *Honey.*

Overachievers

JOIN A DANCING group or club. Perform together. Go to a lake or pool and practice lifting your partner up over your head.

date thirty-five

The Girl Power Date

4+

The Idea

MAKE SURE YOUR guy knows you are not just a girly-girl.

Creative Elements

TAKE YOUR DATE to a cardio kickboxing class, or practice your boxing skills on a punching bag. Lift weights. See who can do the most push-ups at one time. Arm wrestle each other. Play any sport, guys against girls.

Movie Lovers

WATCH *Charlie's Angels* or *Mr. and Mrs. Smith.*

Warning! Don't hurt yourself trying to prove how tough you are.

date thirty-six

The Murder Mystery Date

4+

The Idea

UNLOCK THE MYSTERY together.

Creative Elements

BUY A MYSTERY night kit from any toy store or gaming store, or borrow one from a local library. Send out invitations three weeks in advance and request that your date RSVP. Everyone dresses the part and arrives at the appointed hour. Have dinner prepared, and ask someone's parents or roommates to serve the meal. After dinner, figure out who done it! Play the game *Clue.*

Movie Lovers

WATCH *Clue, Dick Tracy,* or *Minority Report.*

Overachievers

GO TO A dinner theater that involves audience participation.

The Wishing Date

The Idea

LEARN YOUR DATE'S deepest desires, hopes, and dreams.

Creative Elements

A DAY BEFORE, find out what your date's favorite dessert is. Get a roll of pennies from the bank. Go to any area water fountain. Take turns throwing in pennies and saying what you wish for. This is most romantic at night with candles surrounding you. At the end of the activity, have the dessert ready and waiting, and announce that your date's wish has come true. You can add any number of other good lines at a moment like this.

Movie Lovers

WATCH THE MOVIE *Big* or *Pinocchio.*

Overachievers

AFTER LISTENING TO your date's wishes, make one of them come true if possible.

date thirty-eight

The Progressive Dinner Date

4+

The Idea

KEEP YOUR DATE on their toes.

Creative Elements

PLAN AN EVENING of food on the move. Decide on an appetizer, salad, main course, and dessert. This is perfect for a group of four. Each person can be in charge of one item. The idea is to go from one person's house to the next. It's great if each home has music playing in the background, especially if the music complements the meal (Latin music with Mexican food, for example).

Overachievers

DO THE SAME thing, only hopping from one restaurant to another.

The Pretend You're a Tourist Date

The Idea

GET TO KNOW a big city and each other.

Creative Elements

GET A MAP of the city and plan out all the things you want to see and do. Take pictures together in front of monuments. Eat at local cafés or restaurants you've never been to before. Take a horse-drawn carriage ride or a local tour. Visit a museum. Have a meal in the biggest park. Visit a historical site or the home of a famous citizen.

Movie Lovers

WATCH *The Honeymooners* or *The Borne Identity.*

Overachievers

VISIT A BIG city in a neighboring state. Eat at the restaurant with the best reputation.

date forty

The Real Estate Date

The Idea

TO CHECK OUT your date's taste in real estate.

Creative Elements

TOUR HIGH-END MODEL homes, visit advertised real estate open houses, or go see homes for sale. Discuss what you would change if it were your house you were walking through. Describe your decorating style and what colors you most enjoy. Figure out what the monthly payments would be on each home you visit. If you are not sure how to do that, ask the realtor.

Movie Lovers

WATCH *The Haunted Mansion, The Money Pit,* or *Beetlejuice.*

Overachievers

GIVE YOUR DATE a small housewarming gift for a future or current home.

date forty-one

The Taste Test Date

The Idea

SAMPLE NEW FOODS together.

Creative Elements

STOP AT hole-in-the-wall restaurants, diners, or delis you've never tried before. Order one small item to share at each place. Pay attention to the cleanliness, pricing, atmosphere, and staff at each location. Go to Costco and other warehouse grocery stores on sample day. After trying a few new things, buy some favorite items to make each other dinner. Make different foods and feed them to your blindfolded date. Watch a cooking show on TV and try to make what is being taught. Take a cooking class.

Movie Lovers

WATCH *Hitch* or *Simply Irresistible.*

Overachievers

ASK YOUR DATE out again to the restaurant that you felt your date enjoyed the most.

date forty-two

The Homemade Date

The Idea

PLAY AND IMPRESS your date while practicing your homemaking skills.

Creative Elements

DECIDE AHEAD OF time on a do-it-yourself project that you'd like to tackle together. Buy the necessary materials and make it together. A few projects include making a quilt, a bookshelf, a bench, picture frames, an outdoor flower box, a wind chime—any project that sounds like fun. Choose a recipe you have never tried before and make it. Make all parts of the meal, including the appetizer, soup, salad, beverage, main course, vegetables, rolls or bread, and dessert. If possible, use ingredients from your garden.

Movie Lovers

WATCH *Cinderella*.

Overachievers

TAKE ON A more challenging project that lasts for more than one date. Make an impressive dessert ahead of time.

Chapter 6:

Intellectual Dates

date forty-three

The Thinking Date

The Idea

TO PUT A lot of thought into your date.

Creative Elements

SHARE YOUR INTERESTS. Discuss your ideas. List your priorities. Define your goals. Describe your values. Ask each other these ten questions:

1. What color would you never wear and why?
2. If you could make $100,000 a year doing anything for a living, what would you do?
3. What was your favorite movie when you were a kid?
4. If you were lost and alone in the woods, what two items would you want to have with you?
5. Will you be (are you) a Democrat or a Republican or neither, and why?
6. What is your dream vacation?
7. What plays the biggest role in a person's success—education, opportunity, or ambition?
8. Who has had the greatest influence on your life and why?
9. Describe something you wish someone could invent.
10. What do you think about religion?

Movie Lovers

ANY MOVIE THAT makes you think.

date forty-four

The College or University Date

The Idea

LEARN ABOUT, AND take advantage of, the educational tools at your disposal.

Creative Elements

GET BROCHURES ABOUT all the local colleges and universities in your area. Compare the differences in tuition, housing cost, classes and majors offered, professors, and social activities. Take a guided tour of the one you are most interested in. Talk to a professor or adviser in the area you plan to study. Have dinner in the school cafeteria, or have a picnic on the school grounds.

Movie Lovers

WATCH *Rudy, Bio-Dome,* or *A Cinderella Story.*

Overachievers

PICK A CLASS you'd both like to take and sign up during your date.

date forty-five

The Christian Date

The Idea

GO ON A crusade to learn more about Christianity.

Creative Elements

VISIT OR ATTEND a service at a Christian church you don't belong to. Read passages from the Bible together. Borrow books from the library about the history of Christianity. Sing in a choir together. Learn more about the teachings of the great thinkers of Christianity, such as Martin Luther, Joseph Smith, and others.

Movie Lovers

WATCH A MOVIE about the Reformation or *Sister Act.*

Overachievers

BUY YOUR DATE a copy of the Bible and write your feelings in it.

Warning! Always be understanding of others religions. This date is not meant to convert, only to educate.

The Local History Date

The Idea

FIND OUT INTERESTING details about your city, state, and zip.

Creative Elements

GO TO A local library and borrow a book about your hometown or home state. Visit local historical monuments; learn about the first settlers in your area and what they were like. Are you related to any of them? What brought people to your area? Research and watch any movies that cover this topic. Find out how your family came to live in this area. Take a tour of a prominent business in your town, or tour a historic home in your city and learn about the family that lived there.

Overachievers

FIND SOMETHING SPECIAL about your town to show your date, and plan a surprise dinner at that location.

date forty-seven

The Book Date

The Idea

FIND COMMON GROUND, and have creative adventures in good books.

Creative Elements

WITH YOUR DATE, make a list of favorite books. Then each of you make a list of books you'd like to read. Compare notes and see how alike or unrelated your tastes are. Search the web for sites that list classic books, and then pick one you both want to read. Read it and talk about it when you're finished. You could also go to a bookstore and split up to find books that interest you. After ten minutes of browsing, meet up in the café and read together.

Movie Lovers

FIND A MOVIE version of a good book you've never read and watch it. *Pride and Prejudice* and *The House of Mirth* are good choices.

Overachievers

WHEN YOUR DATE chooses a book to read, buy it as a gift.

date forty-eight

The Mormon Date

The Idea

GIVE YOUR ETERNAL companion candidate a pop quiz.

Creative Elements

CAN FOOD TOGETHER at the local family cannery, make someone a meal, or help someone move. Join another couple and teach each other a missionary discussion out of the *Preach my Gospel* manual. Take a walk around a nearby temple. Open GospelLink and search for an interesting gospel topic, or do the same thing on lds.org. Read together the prophet's most recent address. Write in each other's journals. Attend general conference or a baptism. Browse through your local LDS bookstore.

Movie Lovers

WATCH ANY OF the Church Distribution Center videos.

Overachievers

BUY A COPY of *The Book or Mormon* for your date; write your feelings and testimony in it.

date forty-nine

The Buddhist Date

The Idea

HELP YOUR DATE achieve Zen (at least temporarily).

Creative Elements

VISIT A LOCAL monastery. Meditate together. Make bookmarks or visual reminders of some of the wise sayings of Buddha, such as "If you think only of the nonessential, you will never attain the essential." Learn about elephants and their importance to Buddhists.

Movie Lovers

WATCH *Seven Years in Tibet* or *Anna and the King.*

Overachievers

GIVE YOUR DATE an elephant or Buddha figurine.

date fifty

The Biology Date

The Idea

CELL YOUR DATE on your finer qualities.

Creative Elements

TAKE A NATURE hike and point out different foliage and animals that you know. Take pictures of each other with interesting plants and animals in the background. Visit a museum of natural history. Find a book of easy science projects and do one together. Go to a tide pool and see how many sea creatures you can find and identify. Visit a greenhouse and ask for a tour of the different plants. Plant a tree.

Movie Lovers

WATCH *Bio-Dome, Evolution,* or *Red Planet.*

Overachievers

LOOK AT THINGS through a microscope.

Chapter 7:

Manly Dates

date fifty-one

The Backyard Camping Date

4+

The Idea

ROUGH IT WITH a warm house nearby.

Creative Elements

IN YOUR BACKYARD, roast marshmallows, sing camp songs, and tell ghost stories. Set up a guys' tent and a girls' tent. Put up tiki torches, and cuddle under warm afghans. Lie on your backs and look at the constellations. Go for a midnight hike with flashlights. Cook a Dutch oven dinner or dessert. Play lots of silly card games.

Movie Lovers

WATCH *The Parent Trap, The Great Outdoors,* or *Ernest Goes to Camp.*

Overachievers

GUYS SET UP the girls' tent for them.

Warning! Some parents may not approve of both groups sleeping outside. Be prepared with a plan B—the girls sleep inside while the guys sleep outside.

date fifty-two

The Video Game Date

The Idea

LET THE BOYS be boys, and join in the fun.

Creative Elements

PLAY ANCIENT VIDEO games like *Frogger* and *Centipede.* Play *Super Mario Brothers* on a first edition Nintendo. Play team games, such as *Crash Bandicoot, Halo,* or a sporting game. Make things a little more interesting by making the guys play with one hand. Change things up by playing a game on your cell phone or other handheld devices. Eat junk food and drink soda. Go to a game store and pick out a new game to play.

Movie Lovers

WATCH *The Wizard, Cloak and Dagger,* or *Spy Kids.*

Overachievers

GO TO AN arcade or nickelcade.

date fifty-three

The Football Date

4+

The Idea

HAVE YOUR DATE begging to go into overtime.

Creative Elements

PLAY FLAG FOOTBALL in the dark. Play Frisbee football—boys against girls. Have the boys play a game and the girls cheer. Make cookies shaped like footballs. Watch a game on TV. Play a football video game. Play catch with a football. Have a Super Bowl party, and invite other couples.

Movie Lovers

WATCH *The Waterboy, Remember the Titans,* or *Rudy.*

Overachievers

GO TO A professional or college game together; wear face paint and scream your guts out.

date fifty-four

The Gym Date

The Idea

GET YOUR DATE pumped up about being with you.

Creative Elements

GO TO A local gym or fitness center. Work on cardio with treadmills, elliptical trainers, and stair climbers. Work on your muscles with resistance training, and learn about circuit training. Find out what classes are offered and take one together. After you get worn out, sit in the hot tub for a while to relax and unwind. The sauna is also a great way to wind down.

Movie Lovers

WATCH ANY OF the *Rocky* movies.

Overachievers

PLAY A GAME of racquetball or basketball, or join a yoga class. Buy your date a health shake.

Warning! Don't overdo it. If you want the date to last a little longer, try some machines that are low impact.

date fifty-five

The Baseball Date

4+

The Idea

HIT A HOME run with your date.

Creative Elements

PLAY CATCH OR T-ball. Go to a batting cage and practice hitting, or get a group together and play a real game. Have a pop fly contest; see who can catch the most pop flies in a row. Watch a big game together on TV. Wear baseball caps. Eat peanuts and cracker jacks. Practice spitting sunflower seeds.

Movie Lovers

WATCH *A League of Their Own, The Rookie, Field of Dreams, Fever Pitch,* or *Angels in the Outfield.*

Overachievers

GO TO A major league, minor league or college baseball game.

Warning! Remember to bring your mitt to any games; you don't want to get hit by a foul ball.

date fifty-six

The NASCAR Date

The Idea

LET YOUR HEARTS go racing!

Creative Elements

GO TO A go-cart track and race each other, or go to a local speedway and watch novice racers drag race. Buy a set of Matchbox cars and race them down steep places, or dust off some old pinewood derby cars and set up a track to race them on. Play MarioKart on Nintendo. Work on a car. Learn to change the oil and check the tire pressure.

Movie Lovers

WATCH *Guess Who* or *Days of Thunder.*

Overachievers

GO TO A real NASCAR race. See if you can meet with a pit crew or tour the pit area.

date fifty-seven

The Hockey Date

4+

The Idea

MAKE SURE YOUR date isn't hoping for sudden death.

Creative Elements

PLAY ROLLER HOCKEY. Make sure you do a lot of playful body checking. Go to a sporting goods store and try out a pair of rollerblades and sticks. Go to an empty field with a roller-hockey ball and sticks to practice slap shots. Go to an ice arena and practice skating; then try puck handling.

Movie Lovers

WATCH *The Mighty Ducks, Miracle,* or *The Cutting Edge.*

Overachievers

JOIN AN ICE hockey team together. Watch a professional NHL game or college hockey team.

Warning! No fistfights allowed!

date fifty-eight

The Basketball Date

4+

The Idea

MAKE A FAST break with your date.

Creative Elements

WEAR SWEATBANDS, ATHLETIC shorts, and T-shirts, or a jersey from your favorite team. Play HORSE or bump. Play one-on-one, or two-on-two. Do lay up and passing drills, and practice dribbling the ball through your legs. See if you can spin the basketball on one finger like the Harlem Globetrotters.

Movie Lovers

WATCH *Like Mike, Air Bud, Finding Forrester,* or *Love and Basketball.*

Overachievers

TAKE YOUR DATE to an NBA or college basketball game.

Warning! Make sure you wear shoes that will protect your feet and ankles.

date fifty-nine

The Bull's-Eye Date

The Idea

PRACTICE SHOOTING AND see if cupid is a good shot.

Creative Elements

GO TO AN archery range and practice with a bow and arrow or crossbow, or use guns at a gun club, rifle range, or designated area in the woods. Go to an arcade and throw darts at a dartboard; see who can get a bull's-eye first. Play any other shooting games the arcade has, or play duck hunt on Nintendo. Check out guns and bows at a local sporting goods store.

Movie Lovers

WATCH *Robin Hood* or *Robin Hood: Prince of Thieves.*

Overachievers

TAKE A HUNTER'S safety, gun care, or shooting course together.

Warning! Do not attempt these activities unless you have mastered the skills necessary beforehand. Don't be afraid to invite your fathers along on this date.

Chapter 8:

Military Dates

date sixty

The Army Date

The Idea

BE AN ARMY of two.

Creative Elements

GO TO A local army base and take a tour, or dress up in camouflage and go shopping together at the PX. Eat some chow together, and do some physical training, like push-ups and running. Set up an obstacle course and race each other through it. Use walkie-talkies. Learn to disassemble a gun and clean it. Study a topographical map. Learn about the five points of contact. Go online and watch the short Army video about Basic Training. If your date slacks off, make them drop and give you fifty.

Movie Lovers

WATCH *Major Pain* or *Sgt. Bilko.*

Overachievers

PLAY LASER TAG or paintball. Go for a long hike.

date sixty-one

The Navy Date

The Idea

GET TO KNOW each other—full speed ahead.

Creative Elements

TOUR AN AIRCRAFT carrier or cruiser. Play *Battleship*. Peel lots of potatoes. Wear navy blue and white. Watch *JAG*. Make sure your beds are made perfectly; if they're not, make them over together. Give each other a swimming test; see who can hold their breath the longest under water. Put on fins and race.

Movie Lovers

WATCH *Top Gun, Pearl Harbor,* or *Men of Honor.*

Overachievers

TAKE THE NAVY swim test.

date sixty-two

The Physical Training Date

The Idea

GET ROUGH AND tough with your date.

Creative Elements

RUN AT LEAST a mile. Lift weights. Do at least one hundred push-ups, sit-ups, and pull-ups. Learn about different stretches. Figure out what you would have to weigh to get into the military, and challenge each other to get to that weight or better. Work out each major muscle group.

Overachievers

HIRE A PERSONAL trainer for an hour to work with the two of you on your goals.

Warning! Do not overexert yourself trying to impress your date.

The Military Appreciation Date

The Idea

GET YOUR DATE to appreciate you, while appreciating the military.

Creative Elements

WRITE AND SEND letters or care packages to soldiers overseas. Go to a local military base and volunteer. Get a friend or family member who has served in the military to talk to you and your date about their experiences. Tie yellow ribbons on your cars. Visit or volunteer at a veteran nursing home. Visit a local veterans memorial cemetery and leave flowers. Visit a military monument. Discuss your feelings about the military.

Movie Lovers

WATCH *Band of Brothers* or *Life Is Beautiful*.

Warning! Bring some tissue.

Chapter 9:

Outdoor Dates

date sixty-four

The Apple Date

4+

The Idea

MAKE YOUR DATE blossom.

Creative Elements

PICK APPLES AND make a pie or cider. Have a rotten apple fight. Pick apple blossoms and make beautiful bouquets for your mothers. Plant apple seeds together. Eat hot apple crisp at Red Robin, or make your own homemade recipe. Go bobbing for apples. Dip caramel apples.

Movie Lovers

WATCH *The Apple Dumpling Gang.*

Overachievers

SPEND THE DAY working in an LDS welfare apple orchard.

Warning! Watch out for worms.

date sixty-five

The Fishing Date

The Idea

CATCH YOUR DATE—hook, line, and sinker.

Creative Elements

COLLECT LIVE WORMS, or tie flies for fly fishing. Go to a lake, river, stream, or ocean and fish. Learn how to gut and clean a fish. Cook your fish over an open fire, make dip out of it or use it as a stamp for a cool art project. Check out the fish at a local pet store. Go to an aquarium.

Movie Lovers

WATCH *A Perfect Storm, The Great Outdoors,* or *Finding Nemo.*

Overachievers

TAKE YOUR DATE to your private, special fishing hole; have a candlelight dinner waiting when you get there. If you don't catch anything, take your date to a nice seafood restaurant.

date sixty-six

The Hiking Date

The Idea

TELL YOUR DATE to take a hike—with you, of course.

Creative Elements

PICK OUT A local nature hike that you've been meaning to check out near a mountain, forest, river, or waterfall. Pack a lunch and start hiking. Take a compass and create your own trail. Find a stream and follow it to its source. Make homemade trail mix. Try out different hiking boots.

Movie Lovers

WATCH *The Lord of the Rings: The Fellowship of the Ring, The Great Outdoors,* or a *National Geographic* documentary.

Overachievers

PLAN AN ALL-DAY hike with light meals included.

Warning! Make sure you tell people at home where you are planning to go hiking.

date sixty-seven

The Snow Date

4+

The Idea

DATE WHILE WALKING in a winter wonderland.

Creative Elements

BUILD AN IGLOO or snow fort. Go sledding, inner tubing, snowshoeing, or snowmobiling. Have a snowball fight. Take a walk while it's snowing. Make a snowman or snow angels and then make each other hot cocoa. Play hide-and-seek in the snow.

Movie Lovers

WATCH *Ice Age, Elf,* or *The Grinch Who Stole Christmas.*

Overachievers

GO DOWNHILL SKIING, snowboarding, or cross-country skiing.

Warning! Make sure you have the right equipment and skills before heading down a mountain together.

date sixty-eight

The Lost in the Forest Date

4+

The Idea

GET LOST TOGETHER.

Creative Elements

PACK A BACKPACK full of food and head out into the woods. After hiking, take time to stop and eat. Pretend you don't know how to get back, and figure out how you'd survive in the wilderness. Build fires. Build shelters. Find fresh water. Watch the TV show *LOST* when you get back to civilization.

Overachievers

PLAN FOR SOMEONE to come out and rescue you and your date.

! *Warning! Check with local officials for fire hazards and restrictions before starting any fires.*

date sixty-nine

The Raging River Date

4+

The Idea

TAKE YOUR DATE on a wild ride.

Creative Elements

GET LARGE INNER tubes. Have someone drop you off up the river, and arrange for them to pick you up at a certain place and time. Pack some snacks and bottled water, and float down the river together. Surprise your date, and have your driver prepare a special dinner that's waiting for you, along with a change of clothes.

Movie Lovers

WATCH *The River Wild.*

Overachievers

GO ON A white-water rafting adventure together.

Warning! Make sure everyone planning to go can swim. Bring a tube repair kit.

date seventy

The Rock Climbing Date

The Idea

MAKE YOUR DATE hold on for dear life.

Creative Elements

GO TO AN indoor rock climbing facility. After hiking a steep cliff, take pictures of yourself with the view behind you. Climb around on a nearby hill, mountain, or canyon. Research local caves and find an experienced guide to take you inside. Do finger-grip strengthening exercises together.

Movie Lovers

WATCH *Cliff Hanger.*

Overachievers

TAKE A ROCK climbing class together.

Warning! Make sure no one attending this date is afraid of heights.

date seventy-one

The Water Toys Date

4+

The Idea

DRENCH YOUR DATE in attention.

Creative Elements

RENT A CANOE or kayak. Go windsurfing. Rent a paddle-boat and paddle around a nearby lake. Get inflatable mattresses and race. Go wakeboarding, surfing, inner tubing, or sailing. Build sand castles together or bury each other in the sand. Attack each other with Super Soakers. Play in a kiddie pool or on a Slip'n Slide. Run through sprinklers.

Movie Lovers

WATCH *Without a Paddle* or *Overboard.*

Overachievers

GO TO A water park for a day.

Warning! Wear a life jacket.

date seventy-two

The Farm Date

The Idea

SEE IF YOUR date is cut out for country life.

Creative Elements

DRESS IN WORK clothes and gather eggs, feed chickens, milk cows, and plant or harvest crops. Watch the crop dusters fly overhead. Tie or load hay bales. Ride horses. Make cheese or butter. Help prepare the evening meal. Play with baby animals. Kill a pig or chicken for dinner. Look through a *Farmer's Almanac.*

Movie Lovers

WATCH *Babe, Charlotte's Web,* or *Son-in-Law.*

Overachievers

TAKE YOUR DATE for a tractor ride.

Warning! City slickers should stay away from the hindquarters of horses and cows!

date seventy-three

The Zoo Date

4+

The Idea

SOMETIMES IT'S OKAY to be an animal.

Creative Elements

GO TO THE children's section of a zoo and pet the animals. Eat hot dogs. Bring kids along. Take a cool picture with a harmless snake. Check out the exhibits and displays, as well as the animals. Chat with a zookeeper about what it's like to work at a zoo. Take lots of pictures.

Movie Lovers

WATCH *Madagascar.*

Overachievers

ARRANGE TO HELP feed some of the animals.

Warning! Don't feed the monkeys!

date seventy-four

The Doggy Date

The Idea

HAVE SOME FUN with a four-legged friend.

Creative Elements

TAKE YOUR DOG for a walk. If your dog can swim, play fetch in a lake or pond. Take your pet to a doggy park, where it can run around with other dogs, and you and your date can observe and chat. Make puppy prints with paint on paper. Give your dog a bath or haircut together. Run through the sprinklers with your dog. Paint your dog's toenails. Eat hot dogs.

Movie Lovers

WATCH *Air Bud, Lassie,* or *The Fox and the Hound.*

Overachievers

BUY THE DOG a fun, new toy or collar. After all the playing is done, reward Fiddo with a bone to chew on. Go to a dog show.

Warning! Keep your dog on a leash and remember to bring a sack to clean up after it.

Chapter 10:

Pop Culture Dates

date seventy-five

The Harry Potter Date

The Idea

HAVE A MAGICAL evening together.

Creative Elements

LEARN ABOUT J. K. Rowlings. Discuss whom you would live with if both your parents died. Discuss what kind of school you would like to go to. Make a "Marauders Map" of your neighborhood or take a train ride. Dress up like wizards. Eat chocolate frogs.

Movie Lovers

WATCH the *Harry Potter* movies.

Overachievers

BUY YOUR DATE a copy of the latest book in the series.

Warning! This date is really fun if both people have read the Harry Potter books.

The Star Wars Date

4+

The Idea

USE THE FORCE to impress your date.

Creative Elements

WATCH THE *Star Wars Kid* movie online, or listen to the "Star Wars Rap" online. Practice your Jedi skills by playing *Star Wars Monopoly*. Dress up as characters in the movie—girls wear buns on the side of their head. Buy a set of light sabers from a toy store and reenact fight scenes from the movies. Call your date a "scruffy looking nerf hearder" at least once. Listen to the movie sound track in your car.

Movie Lovers

WATCH the *Star Wars* movies.

Overachievers

DISCUSS WHAT KEEPS you from going to the dark side.

date seventy-seven

The Napoleon Dynamite Date

4+

The Idea

MAKE ALL OF your date's wildest dreams come true.

Creative Elements

MAKE BOONDOGGLE KEY chains. Make your date a cake. Make sure you have plenty of Chapstick on hand. Wear moon boots and side ponytails. Help someone with election posters for a campaign for school offices. Eat steaks and *tater tots* for dinner. Try out a dance moves DVD. Drink Gatorade. Ride a bike while pulling your date behind on rollerblades. Take a Tae Kwon Do class. Beat up a piñata.

Movie Lovers

WATCH *Napoleon Dynamite.*

Overachievers

GET GLAMOUR SHOTS taken together. Give your date a copy of the *Napoleon Dynamite* DVD.

The Game Show Date

The Idea

GIVE YOUR DATE the right price on a wheel of fortune.

Creative Elements

WATCH *THE PRICE is Right, Wheel of Fortune,* or *Jeopardy.* Create your own pricing games and come up with fun rewards from a local thrift or dollar store. Each of these game shows has a board game available as well as an online version you can play for free. Play computer versions of your favorite TV game show.

Movie Lovers

WATCH *Quiz Show.*

Overachievers

PURCHASE A NICE item as a prize for the final game.

date seventy-nine

The Internet Date

The Idea

DISCOVER THE WORLD Wide Web together.

Creative Elements

PLAY FREE GAMES online together. Find information about each other's interests. Shop at your favorite online stores. E-mail your friends and family with goofy pictures of the two of you having fun. Look up your next creative date idea on one of the many search engines. Go to a free e-card web site and send out cards to family and friends. Set your screen saver to show a picture of you together.

Movie Lovers

WATCH *You've Got Mail* or *The Net.*

Overachievers

BID ON A gift for your date at Ebay.

Warning! Be careful to block all inappropriate sites on your computer!

The Five Love Languages Date

The Idea

SHOW YOUR DATE you care with words, gifts, service, touch, and time.

Creative Elements

GET A COPY of *The Five Love Languages* and study up on the five love languages. Discuss which language your date speaks and which language you speak. Do things throughout the date that show love in a way that matters most to your date. Prepare a special surprise from each language. Figure out which way you have the hardest time showing love and work on it.

Overachievers

GIVE YOUR DATE a copy of the book.

Warning! This date should be used only by daters who are engaged or married.

date eighty-one

The LDS Movie Night Date

The Idea

GET CAUGHT UP on Mormon pop culture.

Creative Elements

WATCH AS MANY of the following movies as you have time for: *Saturday's Warrior, Charly, Singles Ward, God's Army, Pride and Prejudice, The Other Side of Heaven, The Work and the Glory* movies, *The RM, The Home Teachers, The Best Two Years, Mobsters and Mormons,* and so on.

Movie Lovers

THIS ENTIRE DATE is for you!

Overachievers

GIVE YOUR DATE a copy of one of these movies.

Warning! The humor used in these movies may only be understood if you are LDS.

Chapter 11:

Seasonal Dates

date eighty-two

The Spring Date

The Idea

GET TWITTERPATED.

Creative Elements

LIE ON YOUR backs and watch the clouds roll by; what shapes do you see? Pick flowers and make an arrangement for your home. Visit a petting zoo and hold all the baby animals. Prepare or plant a flower garden. Do some spring cleaning in your yard or house. Pick a home-improvement project and work on it together. Clean out your garage. Go on a picnic.

Movie Lovers

WATCH *Bambi*.

Overachievers

HOLD A GARAGE sale.

date eighty-three

The Summer Date

The Idea

MAKE SURE YOUR date has fun in the sun.

Creative Elements

PLAY FRISBEE AT the park or go for a swim. Make homemade Popsicles. Blow bubbles. Wash a dog outside. Play on a Slip'n Slide. Drink lemonade while swinging on a porch swing. Climb a tree, or fly a kite. Pick berries and make jam. Visit an orchard or a vineyard and pick fresh fruit. Go for a bike ride.

Movie Lovers

WATCH *Weekend at Bernie's, Earnest Goes to Camp,* or *Blue Crush.*

Overachievers

COACH A LITTLE League team. Volunteer together at a local park.

Warning! Whatever you do, don't waste beautiful summer days indoors.

date eighty-four

The Fall Date

The Idea

ENJOY THE BOUNTY of the earth together.

Creative Elements

PICK OUT AND carve pumpkins. Make pumpkin pie. Create a cornucopia or a wreath out of fallen leaves or leaves with fall colors. Take a stroll in the fall leaves with hot apple cider to keep you warm. Rake leaves into a pile and jump in them. Take a drive to a part of your state that has beautiful fall colors. Make a delicious vegetable stew with all the things growing in your garden. Go for a hayride. Bake pumpkin seeds. Make caramel apples.

Movie Lovers

WATCH *The Haunting* or *The Haunted Mansion*.

Overachievers

GO TO A haunted house. Make a scarecrow.

date eighty-five

The Winter Date

4+

The Idea

WARM UP YOUR winter with this hot date.

Creative Elements

SIT BY A warm fire and read good books; share a blanket. Go Christmas shopping together, or make your Christmas lists. Bake cookies and take them to the neighbors. Have a snowball fight. Cut down a Christmas tree and decorate it. Take a drive to look at Christmas lights while playing Christmas music in your car. Go to a soup kitchen, or volunteer to give blankets to homeless people. Go ice skating.

Movie Lovers

WATCH *While You Were Sleeping, Serendipity, Frosty the Snowman,* or *White Christmas.*

Overachievers

TAKE YOUR DATE skiing or snowmobiling.

Warning! Dress warmly!

date eighty-six

The New Year's Eve/Day Date

The Idea

START THE NEW year off right!

Creative Elements

MAKE YOUR LISTS of resolutions and promise to help each other reach your goals. Get dressed up and go to a party or dance. Better yet, throw your own party or dance. Make sure you're near each other at midnight! Wear silly hats and use noisemakers. Drink sparkling cider. Go to your city's New Year's celebration.

Movie Lovers

WATCH *Groundhog Day* or *Dead Poets' Society* and learn about living each day to the fullest.

Overachievers

GIVE YOUR DATE a kiss at midnight, if you dare.

date eighty-seven

The Valentine's Day Date

The Idea

GIVE YOUR VALENTINE a date to remember.

Creative Elements

DECORATE A HEART-SHAPED cake or cookies. Write your date Valentine's Day cards from the grocery store; put them up all over your date's bedroom. Give your date a memento to remember the night by. (My favorite one was from my missionary—he gave me a heart-shaped rock he found on this mission.) Write a list or poem of one hundred things you love about your date, and give it in a pink envelope.

Movie Lovers

WATCH ANY ROMANTIC comedy, like *Sleepless in Seattle, Sweet Home Alabama, The Princess Bride,* or *Hitch.*

Overachievers

GET DRESSED UP and take your date to a fancy restaurant. Have the server bring her a gift on a plate instead of the dessert she ordered.

Warning! Remember who you are!

date eighty-eight

The St. Patrick's Day Date

The Idea

BE THE POT of gold your date has been searching for at the end of the rainbow.

Creative Elements

AFTER SHARING A picnic lunch, search for four-leaf clovers. Wear matching green items. Search "St. Patrick" online and learn all about this Irish man and why there is a holiday named for him. Eat corned beef and cabbage. Make a variety of potato entrées.

Movie Lovers

WATCH *Darby O'Gill and the Little People* or *Far and Away.*

Overachievers

GO TO AN Irish festival. Try doing Irish folk dancing.

date eighty-nine

The Easter Date

The Idea

TO CELEBRATE EASTER together.

Creative Elements

DYE EGGS. PUT together a special basket of goodies and then deliver it to a children's hospital. Set up an Easter egg hunt for your date; use plastic hollow eggs and put slips of paper inside telling the things your date will get for dinner for finding each egg. Some examples might be, "plate," "glass," "salad," "grilled chicken," and so on until you've revealed everything you plan to use and eat with dinner.

Movie Lovers

WATCH THE CLASSIC *The Ten Commandments,* which is on TV every Easter.

Overachievers

CREATE AN EASTER basket and give it to your date at the end of your date. Make your date a traditional Easter feast, or better yet, make it together. Prepare an Easter brunch.

Warning! Remember what Easter is all about.

date ninety

The Mother's Day Date

The Idea

CELEBRATE YOUR DATE'S mom.

Creative Elements

WRITE A THANK-YOU note to your date's mom. Make a breakfast in bed for your moms. Create a game about your mom's life and play it with her. (You could do this with the game *Memory*.) Make your moms a homemade gift together. Invite your moms to a special luncheon that you both plan and prepare.

Movie Lovers

WATCH *Stepmom*, *Monster-in-Law*, or *The Divine Secrets of the Ya-Ya Sisterhood*.

Overachievers

TAKE YOUR MOMS on the date with you.

The Father's Day Date

The Idea

CELEBRATE YOUR DATE'S dad.

Creative Elements

WRITE A THANK-YOU note to your date's dad. Make your dads a tie. Decorate a giant chocolate chip cookie that says, "I love you, Dad! Happy Father's Day!" Plan and prepare everything for a Father's Day barbecue. Take your dads golfing, fishing, or whatever they love to do.

Movie Lovers

WATCH *Father of the Bride.*

Overachievers

TAKE YOUR DADS on the date with you.

date ninety-two

The Fourth of July Date

The Idea

CELEBRATE FREEDOM.

Creative Elements

WEAR RED, WHITE, and blue. Eat apple pie. Listen to the song "I'm Proud to Be an American." Watch fireworks or dance around with sparklers. Have a barbecue. Make and eat red, white, and blue Popsicles. Go to a parade. Invite a date to your traditional family gathering.

Movie Lovers

WATCH *Independence Day, 1776,* or *The Sandlot.*

Overachievers

GIVE SERVICE TO anyone in the service.

Warning! Be safe when playing with fire!

date ninety-three

The Halloween Date

4+

The Idea

CONVINCE YOUR DATE that you're not too creepy.

Creative Elements

CARVE PUMPKINS. HAND out candy to trick-or-treaters. Serve drinks from a punch bowl with dried ice in it. Watch scary movies. Dress up as a famous couple, and go out to a public place in your costumes.

Movie Lovers

WATCH *Signs, Wait until Dark,* or *The Legend of Sleepy Hollow*

Overachievers

TAKE YOUR DATE to a haunted house or other creepy event.

Warning! Scary fun is one thing; don't traumatize your date by doing something too scary.

date ninety-four

The Thanksgiving Date

The Idea

BE THANKFUL FOR time you can spend together.

Creative Elements

MAKE A LIST of the top twenty things you are thankful for and share your lists. Make a cornucopia centerpiece with fresh fruits and vegetable. Dip candles to be used during the big meal. Snack on popcorn. Make or buy a pumpkin pie. Play on the same team during the annual Turkey Bowl. Write each other letters explaining attributes you are thankful for.

Movie Lovers

WATCH *A Charlie Brown Thanksgiving* on TV.

Overachievers

INVITE YOUR DATE to your place for Thanksgiving dinner.

The Christmas Date

The Idea

HAVE A HOLLY jolly Christmas together.

Creative Elements

MAKE GINGERBREAD MEN or a gingerbread house. Go Christmas shopping or ice-skating. Hang Christmas lights together and then warm up with hot cocoa. Decorate your houses together. Make a variety of Christmas cookies and create cookie plates; secretly deliver the plates to your friends and neighbors. Make a snowman. Make a mistletoe decoration with ribbon and artificial plant and pearls. Hang it over your date's door. Make and drink wassail. Get a group together and go caroling or for a sleigh ride.

Movie Lovers

WATCH *Miracle on 34th Street, It's a Wonderful Life,* or *Elf.*

Overachievers

GIVE YOUR DATE a thoughtful gift. Get a photo taken with Santa in the mall together.

Warning! Take it easy with the mistletoe.

Chapter 12:

Service Dates

date ninety-six

The Housework Date

The Idea

SEE IF YOUR date can whistle while you work.

Creative Elements

VACUUM THE CARPET. Dust the pictures. Sweep the tile and hardwood floors. Wash and fold dirty laundry. Beat the dirt out of area rugs. Clean off all countertops. Clean out any yucky food in the fridge, and replace the baking soda box. Wipe out the microwave. Wash and put away dishes. Wash windows. Organize shelves and pantry space. Change linens and make beds. Doing all this work is great because you can learn a lot about your date's skills, work ethic, and natural cleaning habits. You have a chance to talk while you're doing the chores. When everything is spick and span, whoever got their house cleaned pays for dinner or cooks in their newly sparkling kitchen.

Movie Lovers

WATCH *Overboard* and *Snow White.*

Overachievers

BUY AIR FRESHENERS to finish the job. Do all the things listed above, but instead do them for someone in your ward who could use a hand.

The Yard Work Date

4+

The Idea

SEE HOW YOUR date can handle a rake and a wheelbarrow.

Creative Elements

PRUNE HEDGES, mow the lawn, and weed the flower and vegetable gardens. Rake the leaves and jump in the pile. Sweep off steps and walkways. Clean out the gutters. Remove yard waste. When you're finished, depending on what the weather is like, run through sprinklers together or warm up inside with some cocoa.

Movie Lovers

WATCH *Edward Scissorhands.*

Overachievers

DO ALL THE things listed above, but instead do them for someone in your ward who could use a hand.

⚠ *Warning! Have a fun after activity to reward your date for all the hard work!*

date ninety-eight

The Car Wash Date

The Idea

GET TO KNOW your date and your date's car.

Creative Elements

BRING BOTH OF your cars to one person's house. Gather all the supplies needed to wash and service your cars. After washing the exteriors, vacuum the interiors. Clean out any extra items that are cluttering up the cars, and shine the wheels. Check the wiper fluid and oil levels. Check to make sure the tires are properly inflated. Use Armor-all to dust the dashboards. Hang air fresheners inside.

Movie Lovers

WATCH *Shark Tale.*

Overachievers

WAX THE CARS as well. Take your date for a ride in your beautiful car.

The Children's Hospital Date

4+

The Idea

SEE HOW YOUR date reacts to children with special needs.

Creative Elements

ARRANGE TO READ to children at a hospital. Digitally design coloring books to give to the children. Take kids in wheelchairs for a walk. Put on a puppet show or sing a song with the kids. Reassure them that they are special and important just the way they are. Call ahead of time and ask the hospital staff what else you can do that would meet the needs of the children in their care.

Movie Lovers

WATCH *Patch Adams* or *Simon Birch*.

Overachievers

OFFER TO COME back together on a regular basis.

date one hundred

The Environmental Clean-up Date

The Idea

JOIN THE WAR on litter and loneliness.

Creative Elements

DECIDE ON A main road in town and pick up trash. Organize a group of friends to see who can gather the most trash in an hour. Visit a local highway patrol office and have the patrolmen brief you on litter problems in your area that you could help resolve. Collect litter from the edges of rivers, lakes, and ponds in your area.

Movie Lovers

WATCH *Evolution* or *Medicine Man.*

Overachievers

ORGANIZE A GROUP of friends and neighbors to join you!

Warning! Wear gloves, and beware of broken glass.

date one hundred one

The Plant a Tree Date

The Idea

IMPROVE THE ENVIRONMENT, as well as your chances.

Creative Elements

CONTACT STATE OFFICIALS about joining a group that is replanting trees after a clear-cutting. Call a nursery and see if you can get the nursery to donate some saplings. Take whatever trees you can get your hands on to an area that is barren and desolate. Later, you can take pride each time you go past that area, knowing your tree's are there.

Overachievers

BECOME OFFICIAL MEMBERS of the National Tree Trust (800–846–8733) or Trees for Life (316–263–7294).

Warning! Educate yourself before you stick the wrong tree in the wrong piece of earth!

Appendix:

Dating Advice from Elder Dallin H. Oaks

(See "Dating Verses Hanging Out," *Ension*, June 2006, 10–16)

From a May 2005 CES Fireside Address

"THIS TENDENCY to postpone adult responsibilities, including marriage and family, is surely visible among our LDS young adults. The average age at marriage has increased in the last few decades, and the number of children born to LDS married couples has decreased."

"KNOWLEDGEABLE OBSERVERS report that dating has nearly disappeared from college campuses and among young adults generally. It has been replaced by something called 'hanging out.'

"You apparently know what this is, but I will describe it for the benefit of those of us who are middle-aged or older and otherwise uninformed. Hanging out consists of numbers of young men and numbers of young women joining together in some group activity. It is very different from dating.

"For the benefit of some of you who are not middle-aged or older, I also may need to describe what dating is. Unlike hanging out, dating is not a team sport. Dating is pairing off to experience the kind of one-on-one association and temporary commitment that can lead to marriage, in some rare and treasured cases."

"THE CULTURAL TIDES in our world run strongly against commitments in family relationships. . . .

"Whatever draws us away from commitments weakens our capacity to participate in the plan. Dating involves commitments, if only for a few hours. Hanging out requires no commitments, at least not for the men if the women provide the food and shelter."

"SIMPLE AND MORE FREQUENT dates allow both men and women to 'shop around' in a way that allows extensive evaluation of the prospects. The old-fashioned date was a wonderful way to get acquainted with a member of the opposite sex. It encouraged conversation. It allowed you to see how you treat others and how you are treated in a one-on-one situation. It gave opportunities to learn how to initiate and sustain a mature relationship. None of that happens in hanging out."

"MEN, IF YOU HAVE RETURNED from your mission and you are still following the boy-girl patterns you were counseled to follow when you were fifteen, it is time for you to grow up. Gather your courage and look for someone to pair off with. Start with a variety of dates with a variety of young women, and when that phase yields a good prospect, proceed to courtship. It's marriage time."

"MEN HAVE THE INITIATIVE, and you men should get on with it."

"IF YOU DON'T KNOW what a date is, perhaps this definition will help. I heard it from my eighteen-year-old granddaughter. A 'date' must pass the test of three P's: (1) planned ahead, (2) paid for, and (3) paired off."

"YOUNG WOMEN, resist too much hanging out, and encourage dates that are simple, inexpensive, and frequent. Don't make it easy for young men to hang out in a setting where you women provide the food."

"Young women, please make it easier for these shy males to ask for a simple, inexpensive date. Part of making it easier is to avoid implying that a date is something very serious. If we are to persuade young men to ask for dates more frequently, we must establish a mutual expectation that to go on a date is not to imply a continuing commitment."

"YOUNG WOMEN, if you turn down a date, be kind. Otherwise you may crush a nervous and shy questioner and destroy him as a potential dater, and that could hurt some other sister."

"MY SINGLE YOUNG FRIENDS, we counsel you to channel your associations with the opposite sex into dating patterns that have the potential to mature into marriage."

"IF YOU ARE just marking time waiting for a marriage prospect, stop waiting."

"PREPARE YOURSELF for life—even a single life—by education, experience, and planning."

Index

About the Author

LINDSEY SHUMWAY, formerly Lindsey Jex, of Renton, Washington, can appreciate the plight of bored couples. Being raised in a Latter-day Saint home, she was dying to start dating at sixteen. She was so eager, in fact, that for her sixteenth birthday she lined up three dates—one for breakfast, one for lunch, and one for dinner.

After growing discontent with the whole "I don't know, what do you want to do?" routine, she vowed never to waste another date. She developed a reputation for planning fun dates, including watermelon-bowling championships, surprise candlelight dinners in canoes, and her all-time favorite, wishing dates.

Lindsey attended and loved Brigham Young University. After a year of long-distance dating, she married Adam Shumway. Looking back, she says the first thing that caught her attention about Adam was the original pickup line he used on her. (Learn the line on page 6.) The Shumways have been married for seven years and are hoping to go on a Baby Date one of these days, but until then, their two adorable Jack Russell terriers will get to go on lots of Doggie Dates.

0 26575 79339